COERR

Biography of a kangaroo

DATE DUE			
JUL 08			
JUL 28			
OCT 10			
NOV 20			

Missouri Western State College
ST. JOSEPH, MISSOURI 64507

QL
737
.M35
C672

771954

About the Book

At birth the baby kangaroo weighed less than an ounce. But despite his size, he pulled himself upward, groping blindly but instinctively toward his mother's pouch. There, in the darkness, he would taste his first meal and sleep.

Months later Mac would leave the pouch and play with his fellow red kangaroos on the plains of the Australian Great Outback. They had to be ever alert for the eagles, hawks, foxes, and dingoes ready to pounce at any time. Later men with guns would be their only enemy. Full-grown, Mac would weigh 170 pounds and would stand seven feet tall, the steellike muscles of his legs enabling him to speed up to an amazing 35 miles an hour.

Eleanor Coerr's informative text, coupled with Linda Powell's black-and-white illustrations, gives us a vivid picture of the red kangaroos' daily battle for existence on the Australian Great Outback.

Biography of a
KANGAROO

by
Eleanor Coerr

drawings by
Linda Powell

G.P. Putnam's Sons   New York

ACKNOWLEDGMENT

The author wishes to thank Dr. H. J. Frith of CSIRO, Australia, for his assistance.

Text copyright © 1976 by Eleanor Coerr
Illustrations copyright © 1976 by Linda Powell
All rights reserved. Published
simultaneously in Canada by Longman
Canada, Limited, Toronto.
PRINTED IN THE UNITED STATES OF AMERICA
07210
Library of Congress Cataloging in Publication Data
Coerr, Eleanor. Biography of a kangaroo.
1. Kangaroos—Juvenile literature. [1. Kangaroos]
I. Powell, Linda.   II. Title.
QL737.M35C6   599'.2 75-20468
ISBN 0-399-20480-6 ISBN 0-399-60967-9 lib. bdg.

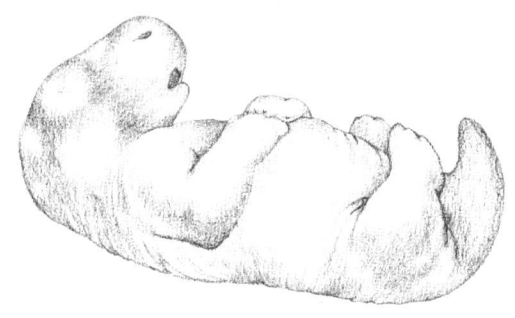

When Mac was born, he was as small as a peanut. His naked pink body weighed less than an ounce. He did not look at all like his four-foot-tall sixty-pound mother, a red kangaroo. In fact, he looked as if he had been born too soon. His tiny hind legs and tail were not quite formed yet. His eyes and ears were shadows underneath a thin layer of skin. Only his forearms were well developed. Each paw had five fingers with strong claws.

Before Mac was born that breezy April afternoon, the marsupial had done all she could to prepare for her baby. Marsupial comes from the Latin word *marsupium*

which means pouch. Each female kangaroo has a pouch that opens like a shirt pocket on her stomach. This mother 'roo had licked the inside of her pouch until it was a clean, safe cradle. Then she had squatted down against a tree with her tail stretched forward between her legs. Mac was born onto the soft underfur of the tail. This was the best starting place for the difficult climb up to the pouch.

Unformed as he was, Mac gripped his mother's fur and pulled himself upward with all his strength. Suddenly,

"SQUAWK! SQUAWK!" A nervous magpie gave a false alarm. The mother 'roo straightened to look around for danger. Mac lost his way in the thick fur. His body was so fragile that he could die if he did not find the pouch quickly. The tiny 'roo groped blindly until instinct and perhaps a sense of smell guided him to the pocket. He scrambled inside.

After his tremendous effort, Mac was weak and hungry. His searching mouth found one of the four nipples and fastened onto it. The nipple began to swell until it filled Mac's mouth. Now he was firmly

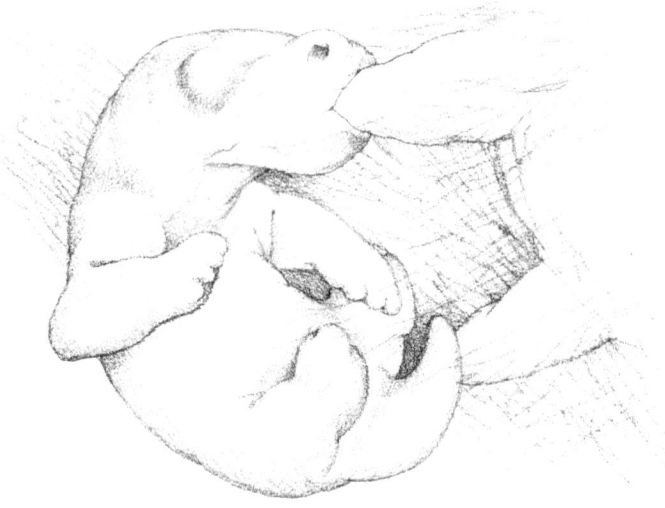

joined to his mother. He lay there in the warm darkness, tasting his first meal. Afterward he slept.

Later his mother gave herself a thorough grooming. Every now and then she stopped to sniff the autumn air. April is

autumn in Australia. She listened to evening sounds with her large twitchy ears. When the mob of kangaroos bounded out onto the open plain to feed, she went along. That night she grazed on tender grass as if nothing special had happened.

For the next five months Mac stayed fastened to the nipple. He woke up, ate, then fell asleep again inside the dark pocket. The only sign of Mac was a swelling in his mother's pouch and an occasional squeak of contentment. He did not know or care about the cool winter days and nights. He was growing and developing so that he would be strong enough to live on the inland plains, Australia's Great Outback, with the other red kangaroos.

In late August, Mac's mouth muscles relaxed so that he could let go of the nipple. He looked more like his mother now. He was covered with a soft smoky blue fur. Later he would change his baby coat for the brick red fur of most adult male red kangaroos. Female red kangaroos remain smoky blue even as adults.

Mac's scientific name, macropod (big foot), fit him well. His feet had grown to be as long as his arms. But his tail was most surprising. It was about four times as long as his arms. He was so active that the pouch humped and bumped as he moved around inside it.

Now Mac became curious about the world and poked his furry head outside. His baby ears were still soft and floppy, but they were as alert as his large brown eyes. The first thing he saw was his mother's gentle face as she bent over to nuzzle him. When he squeaked, she answered with a soft clucking sound. For a while Mac watched her twinkly nose. Then he ducked down and drank her warm milk.

The next time Mac bobbed up, he looked farther than his mother's face. Nearby a few males and young females, called blue fliers, were nibbling the short grass that grew in clumps on the dry land. From his royal perch Mac stared curiously at other joeys. Joey is the Australian name for a baby 'roo.

Mac's bright eyes widened when he saw a huge male that towered above all the others. His muscular body was rusty-red with creamy white fur on his chest and stomach. The seven-foot boomer, a large buck, was one of the strongest and wisest males in the group.

As the joey stretched his neck to get a better look, Boomer suddenly sprang into the air. He landed with such force that his enormous feet slapped the ground with a hard thump. Mac squeaked with fright and disappeared into the safe darkness of the pouch. Boomer had heard the distant roar of a truck. He knew that trucks sometimes carried men with guns. Boomer's thumping warned the other 'roos, and they stampeded in alarm. Mac's mother gave him a bumpy ride as she jolted to earth between soaring leaps.

Soon Mac felt big and strong enough to leave the pouch and bound across the meadows like Boomer. But whenever he tried to climb out, his mother tightened the opening of the pouch with a special muscle in her stomach. Although Mac fussed and squirmed, she kept him there. She knew he was not yet ready to get out.

That time came when he was about six months old. One minute Mac was inside the pocket, and the next he was on the ground. The surprised joey did not know exactly how it had happened, but it was wonderful to stretch every muscle and roll in the fragrant spring grass and flowers.

It was frightening, too. At first nothing seemed to work right. His long tail and big feet got tangled up whenever Mac tried to move. Every few minutes his wobbly legs gave way and he sprawled on the ground. The mother 'roo stayed close by and nuzzled him when he fell.

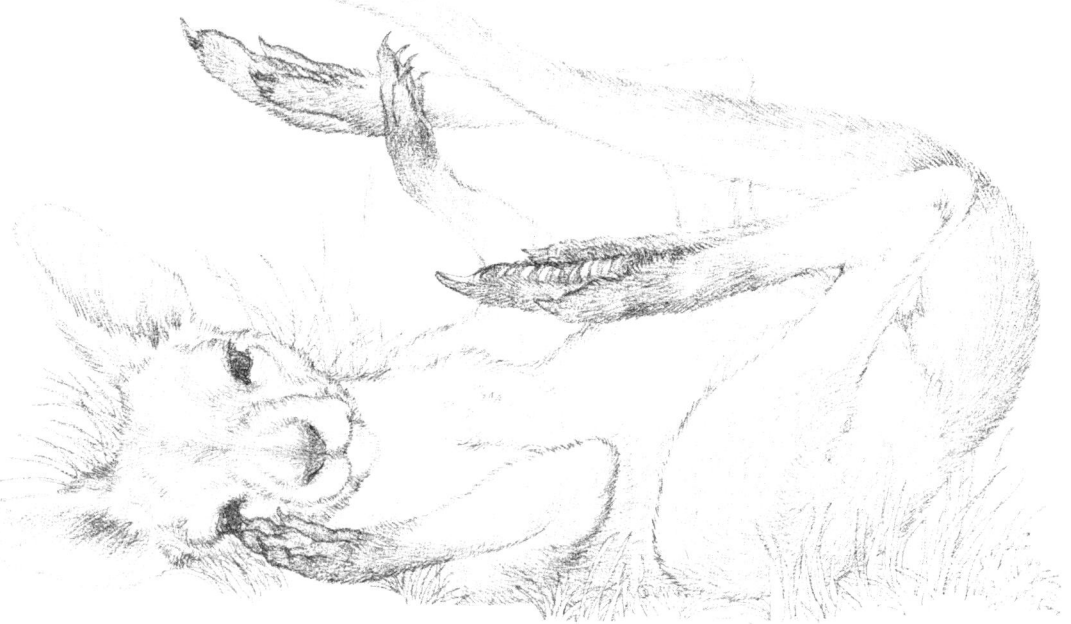

After a few tries Mac was able to walk on all fours. With his front paws and tail firmly on the ground, he swung both hind legs forward in a kind of crawl. Soon he could push off into a hop from the tips of his toes. Now Mac was glad he had such a whopping tail. It steadied him when he crawled. It balanced him like a rudder when he hopped. And it was like a third leg when he sat back on his haunches.

Mac was in and out of the pouch like a little jack-in-the-box. Everything scared him. The weird cackles of kookaburra birds sent him diving headfirst into the

pocket. One of these laughing jacks liked to swoop down and let out an earsplitting shriek near Mac's head. Once inside the safe place, the joey always turned himself around so that he could peek out and see what had frightened him.

The doe was a good mother. Taking care of an active young joey was hard work, and she had no help from Mac's father. After a male 'roo mates with a female, he shows no interest in her or their offspring.

As soon as the sun dried the early-morning dew, she tipped Mac out for his daily scrubbing. While he struggled and complained, she licked and combed his fur until every hair was glistening. Patiently she let Mac play with her ears, pull her tail, and swat her nose. When she

tried to rest, the little fellow was never still. She managed to doze in short naps with her eyes half closed to keep any harm from coming to her baby.

It was a relief for his mother when Mac began to play with the other joeys during the long warm afternoons. While the adults lay on their sides in scooped-out shallow nests under the gum trees, the young ones romped nearby. The smallest joey in the mob was a real sleepyhead.

Every now and then Sleepy would stop playing and put his head down on his paws for a catnap. One of the older joeys was always spoiling for a fight. His punches and kicks were so rough that Mac crawled into his mother's pouch and stayed there until Fighter went away. For the moment Mac was content to watch Boomer and the other males wrestle and box.

Mac especially liked the water hole called a billabong. Sometimes the 'roos joined flocks of birds that whirred to the billabong for an evening drink. From their mothers' pouches Mac and Sleepy had a great time splashing and dabbling in the water. Cranes and grave pelicans drank quietly a safe distance from the noisy joeys.

The doe was nervous whenever Mac was out of the pocket. She knew there was danger in the Great Outback for baby 'roos. In the daytime hungry eagles and hawks waited for a chance to pounce on unprotected joeys. At night foxes and wild dogs called dingoes prowled silently through the darkness looking for food.

Also, there were men with guns. Some hunters shoot 'roos for meat and skins. Others are hired by ranchers who believe that kangaroos take food and water away from their sheep and cattle. Some men even kill the wild creatures for fun.

The sky was blazing with an orange sunset when the mob dashed off to the open fields where they would graze most of the night. After sniffing the air, listening, and looking all around, the mothers

let their youngsters out. Mac nibbled at a few tender shoots, then washed them down with lots of milk. Mostly, he wanted to play. He bounced around his mother trying to swat the perky Willy Wagtail that perched on the doe's back. The little black and white flycatcher was waiting to nab insects that flew up from the grass when the 'roo grazed.

Mac and Sleepy had just started a rough-and-tumble game when their mothers became alarmed. They saw two wedge-tailed eagles circling in the sky. At once the does made frantic sucking sounds to call their young. They leaned forward so the joeys could rush into their pouches. Mac's mother whisked him off to safety. But Sleepy moved too slowly.

One huge eagle swept down between him and his mother. It beat at the doe with powerful wings to keep her separated from her joey. The other bird landed behind a bush and sneaked up behind Sleepy. In a flash it grabbed the young 'roo in its strong talons. The first eagle joined its partner to kill and eat their prey. Sleepy's mother could do nothing.

For a while Mac stayed closer to his mother. If they became separated, he chittered anxiously and went up to each female until he found the right one. He was so big now that he could scarcely squeeze all of himself into the pocket. He still slept, suckled milk, and traveled in it even though he was a hefty sixteen pounds. Most of the time his hind feet stuck up out of the opening alongside his head.

One day Mac found a strange thing waddling across the dirt. As he poked at the lizard, a curious emu came over to

have a look. When Mac turned and saw the five-foot-tall flightless bird standing over him, he took off. Without looking where he was going, the joey dived at the

nearest stomach. It belonged to Boomer. Casually the buck brushed Mac aside. He tumbled over backward in his hurry to reach his mother.

And then a strange thing happened. His mother stood tall and closed the pouch so that Mac couldn't get in. Mac buried his face in his mother's fur until the emu sped back to the others.

Later that day Mac ran to his mother for his usual ride out to the open plain. Gently she pushed him away. Mac tried to pull the pouch open with his paws. Again she pushed him away. Clucking for

Mac to follow, the doe set out after the mob. Mac sat back on his tail and squeaked unhappily. But when he saw his mother hop farther and farther away, he followed her. She stopped often so that her little joey could keep up. When they reached the field, Mac's tender feet were tired and sore. He longed to cuddle down in the warm pocket for a rest, but it was someone else's cradle now.

A tiny sister had been born and was snugly fastened to another nipple. She drank a special thin milk while Mac's nipple still provided the rich milk his bigger body needed. For about five more months the mother 'roo would let Mac poke his head into the pouch to suckle. Then he would be on his own.

This was a dangerous period for Mac. At eight months he was still small enough to be killed by the Great Outback predators. And he had no place to hide. His survival depended on caution and his powerful legs. An eerie birdcall, the howl of dingoes, or the scream of some small animal under attack sent Mac scooting to his mother's side. The touch of her nose on his made him feel safe.

Mac was an alert youngster. He began to mimic everything his mother did. When she lifted her nose to sniff for danger, Mac did too. He pricked up his ears to listen when she did. His ears had grown erect, and he could move them this way and that to catch the faintest sound. When his mother zipped away at the snap of a twig, Mac followed as fast as he could go. He never stopped to see what was chasing him. He just ran.

He learned where to find the mixture of green and dry short grasses and herbs that a 'roo needs. His new teeth were perfect for cropping grass. The front ones were sharp and long for cutting off shoots close to the roots. Broad molars did the grinding.

Mac was growing up fast. His baby fur began to shed. In its place grew the orange-red coat of the male yearling. From now on he would grow new fur every year. When he stood on tiptoe, Mac was almost as tall as his mother. He would stop growing at about eight years of age. Females slow down at two and stop growing when they are four.

Mac was also braver. He no longer hid from Fighter. The two young 'roos often wrestled and played together. Then one day Fighter flicked his paws at Mac, and they began to box. Mac let out a startled grunt when Fighter socked him smartly on the nose. For a moment Mac steadied himself on his strong tail. At once Fighter landed a series of clouts on Mac's chin. Biff! Pow! Mac reeled against a tree. Like most males, Fighter was polite when play-boxing. He seemed to step back between rounds and wait for Mac to get his breath. Neither really won, but it was fun and good practice. Mac would have to fight other bucks for a mate when he was older. And he would surely have to fight dingoes.

After each boxing match, Mac sat back on his hindquarters to groom himself. He copied Boomer's grooming habits. First Mac gave himself an all-round scratching with his clawed paws. Then he used his feet. Of his four toes, the two inside ones had nails that were perfect for combing tangled fur. He could even clean his ears with the curved razor-sharp nail on the big center toe. Mac finished by licking his paws and washing his face like a cat. Except for an occasional roll in the dirt to discourage insects, Mac kept his fur glossy and clean.

In the winter a third baby was born to the mother 'roo. Mac's little sister was forced to stay out of the pouch just as he had been. Mac enjoyed playing with her, although female kangaroos don't box or wrestle. What they lack in strength and size, they make up in speed.

It seemed that the mob had found the perfect place to live. So far no 'roo hunters had come into their area, and there was plenty of food and water.

That changed when summer came. In January the weather turned unbearably hot. Day after day a coppery sun steadily burned the land. Every night the 'roos traveled miles to search for food. Large marsupials can go for many days without water, but they must have food. Mac's little sister became so weak that she fell down and couldn't get up. She died of starvation. Scattered across the plain were dead rabbits, sheep, cows, and a few kangaroos. Predators were busy day and night doing their cleanup job for nature.

Mac had no time or energy for play now. Red-eyed and weary, he constantly nosed the ground for tiny dust-covered shoots of grass or any pockets of dew. Sometimes he got so warm that he licked his arms and chest. When the saliva evaporated, he felt a little cooler.

One evening Mac saw Boomer leap over a fence that was too high for the other 'roos. The buck had caught the scent of water near a rancher's home. Boomer never came back. The rancher was saving that water for his sheep. He shot any thirsty animals who came near.

In the middle of a stifling hot afternoon Mac tensed and sat up, his nose twitching. He smelled a storm coming. The sky became dark, and thunder echoed across the land. A few drops plopped onto the parched earth; then the rain pelted down.

Mac and his mother huddled together under a spindly coolabah tree. They eagerly lapped up the rainwater that gathered in a puddle at their feet.

In a short time the fields were spotted with patches of green. Brightly colored birds filled the air with their songs. Life in the Great Outback returned to normal. The 'roos grew fat and frisky again. Now that there was a good supply of food, the adult 'roos mated.

Mac and Fighter were wrestling one cool autumn night when they heard a strange sound miles away. Something was coming, something noisy and dangerous. Mac stood tall on his hind legs, keen nose and ears into the breeze. The sound grew louder. It was the roar of motors and bang of guns.

Instantly the 'roos rushed to get away, every animal for himself. The swift blue fliers were soon ahead of the heavier males. Mac leaped higher and higher, faster and faster.

Suddenly a bright searchlight swept across the field. Fighter stopped and turned to face the enemy. It was a fatal mistake. Professional hunters in a jeep dropped him with a bullet. Several other 'roos were caught in the blinding glare of the light and killed. Mac whizzed on. He did not know that his mother was slowed down by the weight of the baby in her pouch. In a final desperate move she slipped the joey out into a bush and flung herself forward in a burst of speed. It was too late. She was shot. Toward morning a hungry fox found the baby 'roo.

Mac did not stop running until he was far away. He did not see the hunters put the 'roo bodies into refrigerated boxes

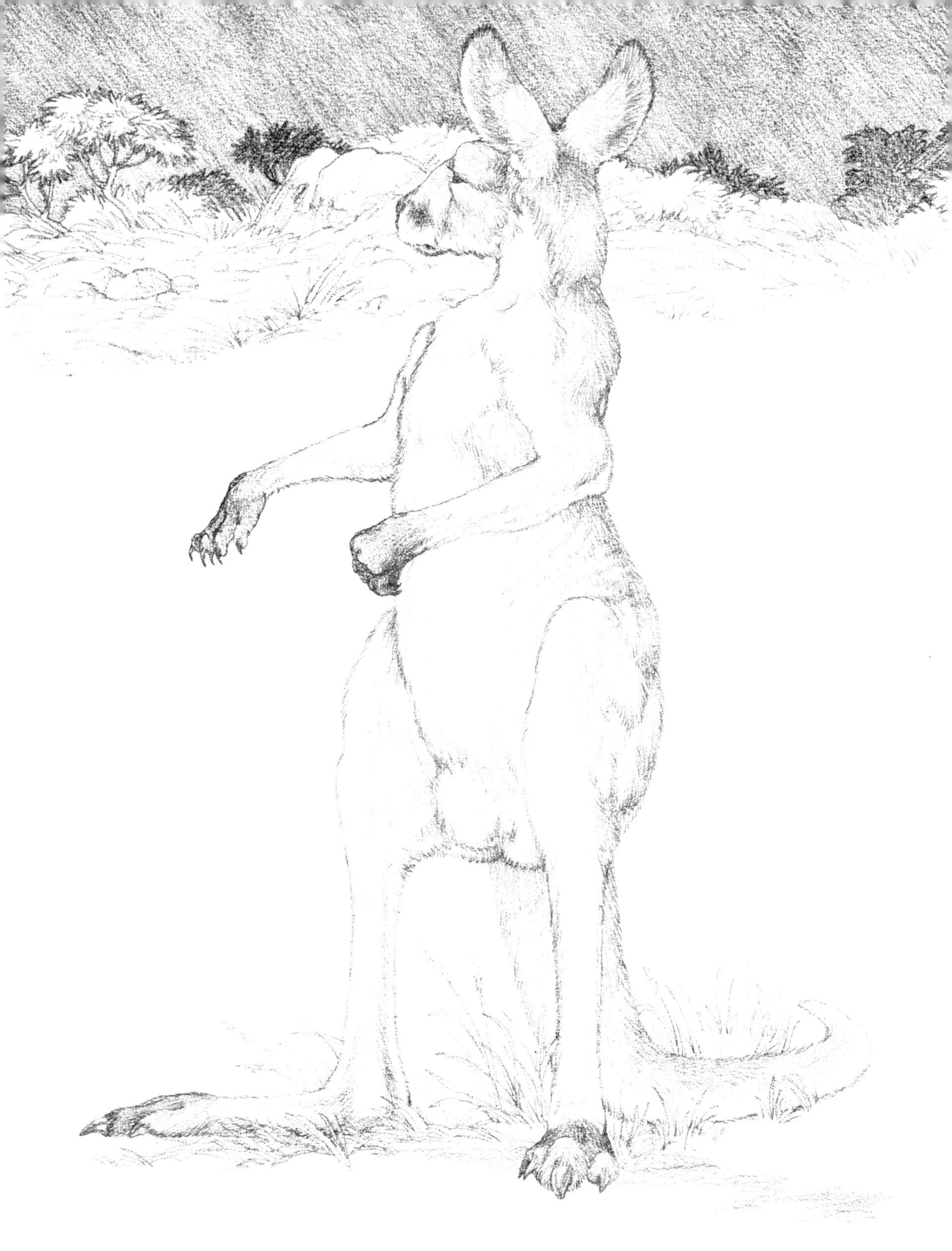

called chillers. Later the chillers would be taken to the city. The meat and hides would be used for pet food and leather articles.

When the sky lightened, what was left of the mob was scattered far and wide. Mac was alone.

For the next few years Mac joined one small group of 'roos and then another. Since he was still too young to mate, the other males welcomed him. He lazed away the warm afternoons dozing in the shade. In cool weather he grazed both day and night, resting out in the fields. When he wanted to box, there was always a young buck nearby ready for a friendly fight.

Like most 'roos Mac was gentle and peace-loving. But if he was cornered, he fought bravely. Sometimes he had to fight dingoes. Mac had a special way to deal with them. He simply held a wild dog in a tight bear hug close to his chest while he lashed upward with a well-aimed kick. If many dingoes attacked near a billabong, Mac waded chest-deep into the water. When a dog swam out, Mac clasped him in his arms and drowned the unfortunate animal. One by one, he conquered them.

As Mac grew larger, his only real enemy was man. There was just one way to deal with him—run! Mac's alertness and the steellike muscles in his legs always saved him from the hunters.

Four-year-old Mac was cropping grass under a jumble of stars one night when a pleasing new scent drifted toward him. A dainty young blue flier hopped by. She was ready to mate. Mac sprinted toward her. They touched noses, and Mac made gentle sucking noises. While he courted her, another buck raced up to them.

Nervously Mac licked his arms and chest. He whirled to face his competition. The males coughed raspingly and began to grapple. The stranger reared up on his stiffened tail and kicked hard with both feet. Mac twisted out of reach. He strained every muscle to kick or push

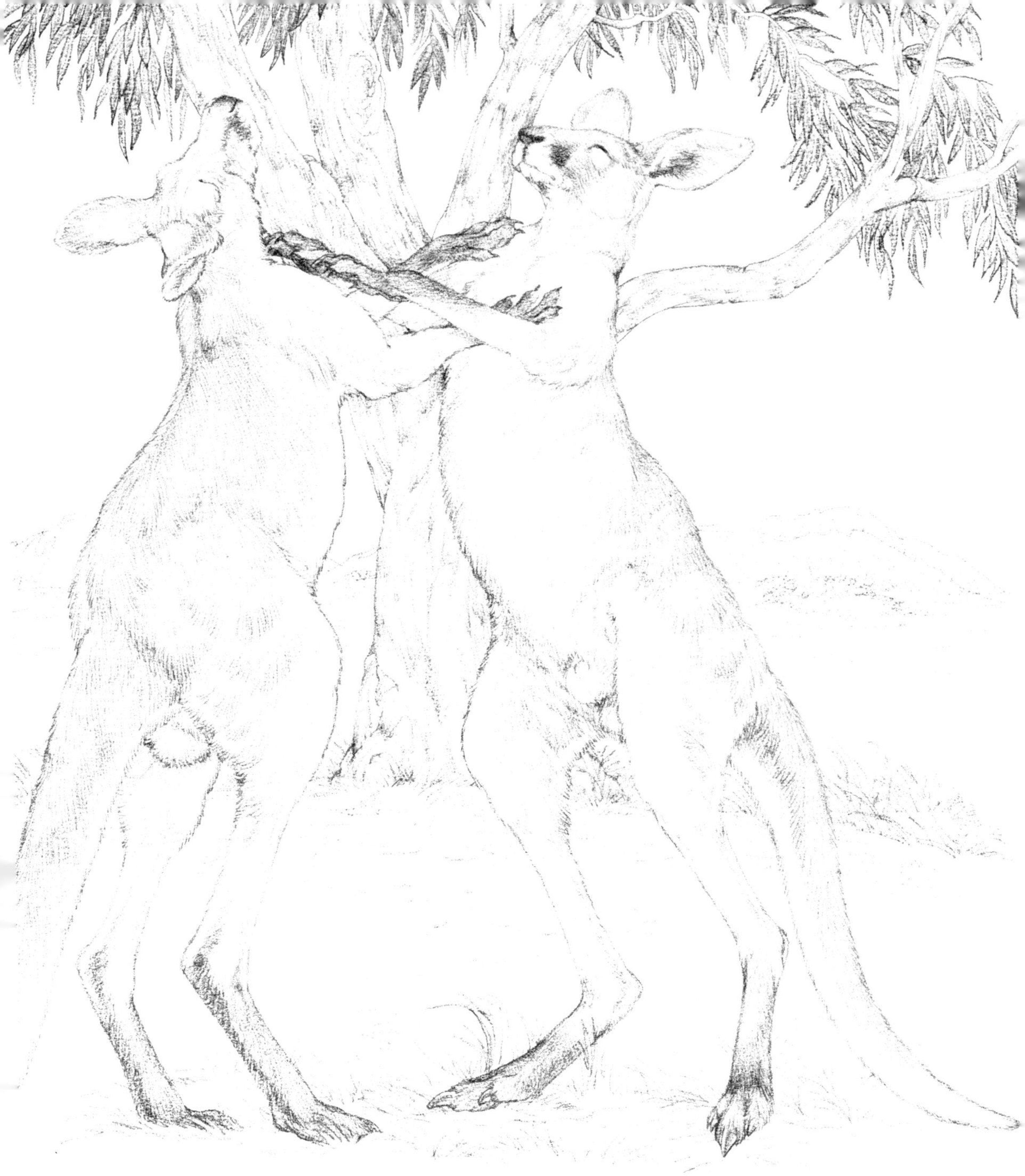

over the other male. Finally Mac was able to bring up a hind leg in a lightning-fast motion. The terrible nail on his large toe caught the enemy on the thigh. The fight was over. The other 'roo crept away to nurse his bleeding wound.

Mac was exhausted. One ear was torn, and he ached all over. But he had won his first mate. He led the blue flier to a billabong to drink and rest. He sensed that something was not quite right. The water hole was surrounded by a high fence that glinted in the moonlight. Mac slowly went around the barrier until he found an opening. It seemed safe, so he went through. The blue flier followed. Mac dipped his arms and shoulders into the cool water as he drank.

Suddenly Mac lifted his head. A faint shift in the breeze brought him the dreaded scent of man. Out of nowhere a dazzling light shone directly into Mac's eyes. He froze, blinded by the glare. Before he knew what was happening, he was grabbed roughly from behind.

"Get his tail!" a voice shouted.

"Stay behind him!" another yelled. "This is a big one."

Strong arms encircled Mac's neck. He struggled desperately, but husky men threw him to the ground. They held Mac fast and fastened something around his neck. At the same time others were handling the timid blue flier.

As suddenly as the attack came, it was over. Mac and the blue flier found themselves free in the darkness. They leaped through the gate and raced for the open.

In the dim morning light Mac saw a bright collar around his mate's neck. His

paws felt something smooth and cold around his neck, too. No matter how hard he tried, he could not paw it off. It was a two-inch-wide plastic collar. On it were two red diamond shapes, a purple triangle and a green square. Hanging from the collar was a metal disk with a number on it. These would identify Mac wherever he went for the rest of his life.

The billabong was a banding station run by the Australian government. By tagging red kangaroos, scientists hope to learn more about their movements and numbers.

Mac did not stay long with the blue flier. About thirty-three days after their mating she gave birth to the first of Mac's many sons and daughters. But Mac took no part in family life.

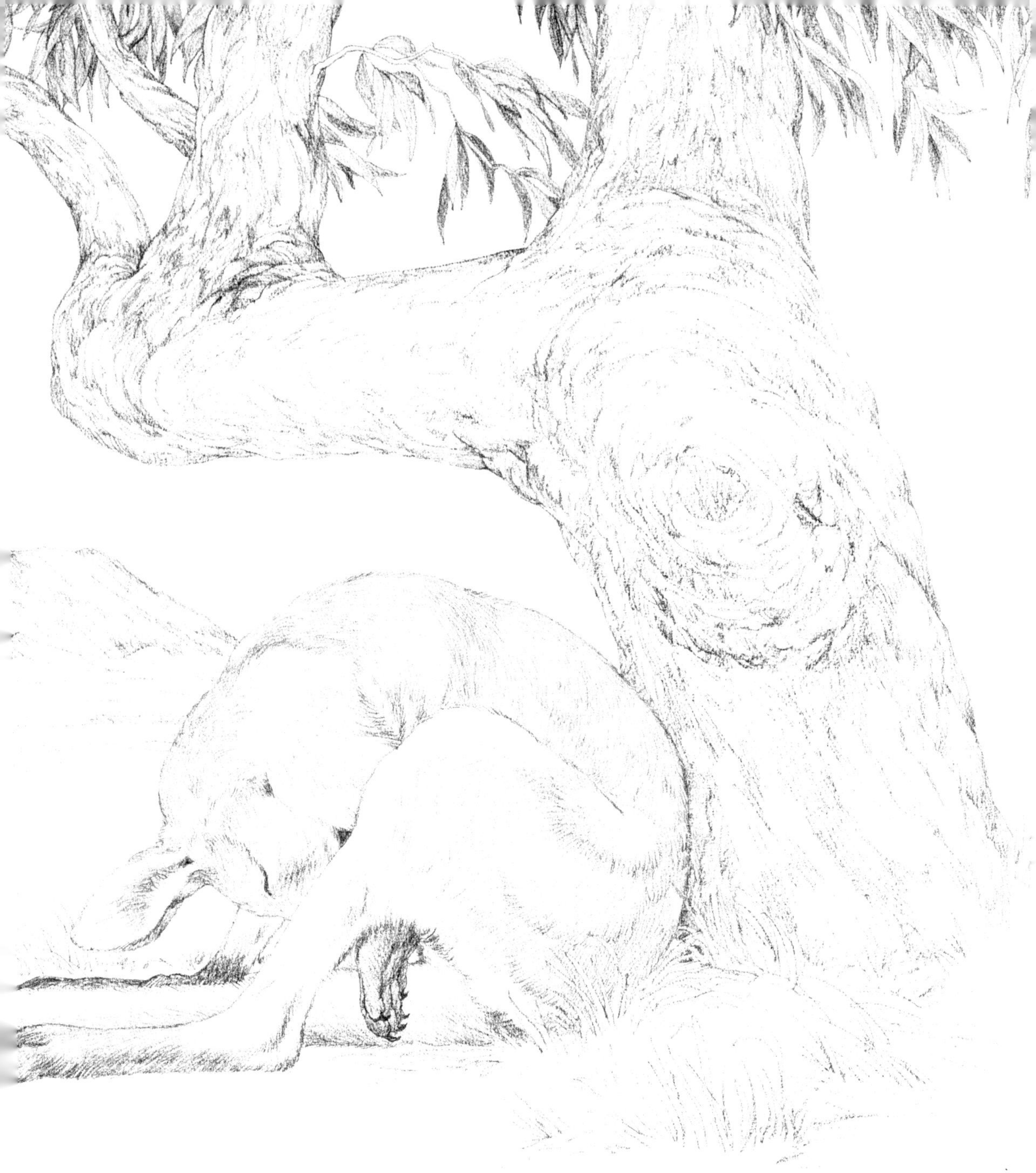

Year after year Mac roamed the Great Outback, always finding the best grazing land. When he finished growing, he weighed close to 170 pounds and was a strapping seven feet tall. As he raced across the open land, his movements flowed smoothly like those of a trained athlete. He could soar in leaps four feet off the ground and jog along at 15 miles an hour. When he wanted to lose a pursuer, Mac could burst forth at a speed of 35 miles per hour. With his head and tail up, paws tucked in, Mac in full flight was spectacular.

Now he was a boomer. Whenever he sensed danger, Mac warned the other 'roos with his thumping feet. If he stayed healthy and alert, Mac would probably live to the ripe old age of fifteen.

About the Author

Eleanor Coerr was reared in Saskatchewan, Canada. After she received a BA from the American University in Washington, D.C., she began to write newspaper columns for children. She has traveled widely and started the first public library for children in Ecuador, a project which prompted her to get an MA in library science.

This is Eleanor Coerr's second Nature Biography for Putnam's. The first was Biography of a Giant Panda.

About the Artist

Linda Powell was brought up and educated in California. After receiving a degree in fine arts from the Art Center College of Design in Los Angeles, she moved to Colorado, where she now works as an assistant art director. Ms. Powell, a member of the Audubon Society, has many interests, among them tropical fish and animals. She has designed numerous cards, posters, calendars, and books.